Longman Keys to Language Teaching

Mistakes and Correction

Longman Keys to Language Teaching

Series Editor: Neville Grant

Mistakes and Correction

Julian Edge

Longman

London · New York

Addison Wesley Longman Limited
Edinburgh Gate, Harlow
Essex CM20 2JE, England
and Associated Companies throughout the world.

Distributed in the United States of America
by Longman Publishing, New York

First published 1989
Sixth impression 1996

British Library Cataloguing in Publication Data

Edge, Julian
   Mistakes & correction. – (Longman keys to language
   teaching).
   1. Educational institutions. Curriculum subjects:
   English language. Teaching
   I. Title
   420′.7

Library of Congress Cataloging in Publication Data

Edge, Julian, 1948–
   Mistakes & correction/Julian Edge.
       p.   cm. – (Longman keys to language teaching)
   Bibliography: p.
   ISBN 0-582-74626-4
   1. English language – Study and teaching – Foreign speakers.
   2. English language – Errors of usage.   I. Title.   II. Title:
   Mistakes and correction.   III. Series.
   PE 1128.A2E28 1989
   428′.007 – dc19

ISBN 0582 74626.4

Set in 10/12 Century Schoolbook

Produced through Longman Malaysia, TCP

The publishers are grateful to the following for their
permission to reproduce copyright material:

L. Jones, "Functions of English" pub. Cambridge University
Press for page 40; K. Morrow and K. Johnson, "Communicate
1" pub. Cambridge University Press for page 42 and M. Swan
and C. Walter "Cambridge English Course" pub. Cambridge
University Press for page 44.

Contents

Preface

The *Longman Keys to Language Teaching* series is intended especially for the ordinary teacher. The books in this series offer sound, practical, down-to-earth advice on useful techniques and approaches in the modern ELT classroom. Most of the activities suggested in these books can be adapted and used for almost any class, by any teacher.

When this series was being planned, high on the list of priorities was a book on mistakes and correction in language teaching. While I was teaching with Julian Edge on a British Council Summer School for teachers in Tokyo recently, this was an area that interested us all very much, and it became clear that he was just the person to write this book.

There was a time, not so long ago, when the main question we asked ourselves about learners' mistakes concerned how to prevent learners from making them. This book is concerned with much more interesting questions: *when* to correct mistakes – and when not to; and *how* to correct them.

Recently there has been an increasing realisation of the important role mistakes have in the learning process. This book examines this role, particularly with a view to encouraging communicative fluency, rather than merely mechanical accuracy. The book suggests many practical techniques for helping our students to accept and learn from their mistakes without being discouraged by them.

Neville Grant

To Ingrid, die Nettigste

Acknowledgements

It is impossible to acknowledge all the individuals, teachers, colleagues and students, from whom I have learned the ideas and techniques that I try to pass on in this book. Where I can relate a technique directly to an individual, it then seems invidious to do so. Thank you all.

My special thanks to Neville Grant, for much support and one or two of the weaker examples (smile).

Introduction: a question

Most people agree that making mistakes is a part of learning.
Most people also agree that correction is a part of teaching.

If we agree so far, then we have an interesting question to answer:

> If making mistakes is a part of learning, and correction
> is a part of teaching, how do the two of them go
> together?

This is the question we shall try to answer in this book.

In Chapters 1–3, we look at different types of mistake. We also see
why mistakes are so important in language learning. In Chapters
4–7, we ask when it is useful to correct, and look at different ways
of correcting. Chapter 8 discusses the teacher's own English.
Finally, we attempt an answer to our main question.

At the end of each chapter, there are a number of questions and
activities. These will usually be most useful if you first do them by
yourself and then talk about them with a colleague.

Questions and activities

1 Think of something in your life that you have learned to do. Can
   you think of a mistake that you made which helped you to
   learn? How did it help?

2 Is it part of the teacher's job to make sure that everything said
   in class is correct all the time?

3 Think about your own experience of learning a language and of
   being corrected. How did your teachers correct you? How did you
   and your classmates react? It's important to remember our own
   experiences and also to remember that not everyone is like
   ourselves.

Mistakes of meaning

When we use the word *mistake* in a general sense, we all know what we mean by it. When a teacher says, 'These exercises are full of mistakes,' or, 'Their writing is good, but they make lots of mistakes when they speak,' we have no difficulty in understanding what the teacher means. But if we look carefully at the mistakes our students make, and the mistakes we make ourselves, we find that the general term *mistake* covers many different things that happen in language use. In this chapter and the next, therefore, we shall try to separate out some different meanings of *mistake*. Then, in later chapters, we can look at suitable types of correction.

> The most important sort of mistake is a mistake that leads to a misunderstanding.

Imagine a student, Cheng, who wants to buy a jacket in Britain. She goes into a shop and says,

Please will you to show me coats?

What is the most important mistake here? I think the most important mistake is that she says *coats*, because this will lead to a misunderstanding. *Will you to show me* is not correct English, but it is polite and easy to understand, so this mistake is not so important.

What is the most important mistake in the following conversation?

Peter: How long are you here for?
Amira: Two years.
Peter: Wha . . .! You are already here since two years?
Amira: No, no, I am come yesterday.
Peter: Oh, yester . . .
Amira: No, no, last week, I mean I came last week.

I would say that the most important mistake occurs in Peter's first question, because this causes a misunderstanding. The question:

How long are you here for?

usually refers to the future, and this is what Amira responds to. What Peter really wanted to ask was:

How long have you been here?

He chose the wrong verb form and that caused the misunderstanding.

Peter's question looks perfectly correct in a linguistic sense, but the problem is that it doesn't mean what he wanted to say.

> There is no point in learning to say correct sentences in English if they don't mean what we want to say.

So, although Peter's use of *since* and Amira's use of *am come* are certainly mistakes, they are not as important as Peter's wrong choice of verb tense in the first sentence, because they are unlikely to lead to a misunderstanding. What can we learn here?

> A teacher's job in hearing mistakes is more difficult, and more interesting, than just listening for incorrect forms of language.

Now, imagine a customer, Nesrin, going into a shop in an English-speaking country. What are the important mistakes here?

Nesrin: Good morning.
Shopkeeper: What can I do for you?
Nesrin: Give me two apples.

(Shopkeeper weighs two apples, puts them in a bag and gives them to Nesrin)

Shopkeeper: Anything else?
Nesrin: No. How much this?
Shopkeeper: Forty pence.

(Nesrin pays and leaves.)

Nesrin finds the shopkeeper impolite because he does not return her first greeting. The shopkeeper finds Nesrin impolite for not saying 'please' or 'thank you'. As far as their own backgrounds are concerned, each of them has been behaving properly and the other person has been impolite. This is a really important area of misunderstanding.

People don't usually mind if foreigners make grammatical mistakes such as,

How much this?

but people are not very forgiving of social mistakes such as,

Give me two apples.

Even if they know that the person speaking is still learning the language, people everywhere tend to think that their own forms of politeness are somehow 'natural'. In this example, Nesrin gets her apples, but such misunderstandings might make it very difficult for two people to get on with each other.

We have looked so far at two sorts of mistake:

- the mistake that occurs when a speaker uses a correct piece of language (linguistic form) that doesn't mean what the speaker wanted to mean;
- the mistake which occurs when the speaker uses a correct linguistic form which is socially unacceptable — the big problem here being one of politeness.

As teachers, we can learn:
- not to rush into correction before we know what someone wants to mean, and
- to think about politeness as well as correctness.

When teachers talk about mistakes, they usually mean mistakes of linguistic form. Here, too, we should concentrate on mistakes that affect meaning and communication.

In doing this, we can see that some mistakes are more important than others. For example:

Are you come here yesterday?

The first part of the sentence is difficult to interpret, but as soon as we hear *yesterday*, we have no trouble in understanding what is meant.

Some mistakes have a much wider effect:

Some people think the mountains is the best place for the holiday. On the contrary, the seaside is the favourite place for most of the people.

What does this mean? Did the writer want to say something different in the first sentence, or something different in the second sentence? Or is the mistake in the use of *On the contrary* itself? Did the writer mean *On the other hand*? If so, we can see that this mistake affects the whole of what the writer says, because it is difficult to follow what was meant. Is the second sentence supposed to contradict the first sentence or not?

> It is more important to correct mistakes which affect the meaning of several sentences than to correct small grammatical points inside one sentence.

In this chapter, we have emphasised meaning and communication. We have also seen that meaning and communication are affected by mistakes of language form. So, in the next chapter, we go on to look more closely at mistakes of form and see what different types we find there.

Summary

1 The most important mistakes are those which affect meaning and communication.

2 Correct linguistic forms are of no use if they don't mean what we want to say.

3 When we talk to people, being polite is more important than being linguistically correct.

4 Mistakes that affect a long stretch of language are more important than mistakes which have only a local effect.

Questions and activities

1 Think of an occasion when you said something in a foreign
language which was misunderstood. Was the misunderstanding
caused by a grammatical mistake? Were there other causes?

2 Think of a misunderstanding when someone else was speaking.
What factors caused the misunderstanding?

3 Think of an occasion when a misunderstanding took place
between people speaking their own language. What caused it?

4 Can you remember a time when someone sounded impolite
when speaking a foreign language – perhaps when a foreigner
was speaking your language? Do you think they were impolite,
or was it a case of differences in normal behaviour?

5 Can you find some mistakes in students' writing which affect
the meaning of more than one sentence?

Mistakes of form

When we talk about mistakes of form, we are comparing something in the student's English with standard English. For example, if a student says,

I am came yesterday.

we would probably compare that with the standard form,

I came yesterday.

and call it a mistake.

Now let's go further and look at what causes mistakes, and then at a teacher's view of different types of mistake.

Causes

- One cause of mistakes in speaking a foreign language is the influence of the speaker's first language.

We can usually hear this, for example, in the pronunciation of the language. That is why we say that we can tell where someone comes from by their accent. Many Spanish speakers, for instance, have difficulty with words which start with *st*. Instead of 'star', they tend to say, 'e-star', as in:

Look at the beautiful e-stars!

We can also notice the influence of the first language in the vocabulary and grammar of learners. Sometimes this is deliberate, sometimes not. When people don't know how to say something in a foreign language, one possibility is to use words and structures from their own language and try to make them fit into the foreign language. A German speaker with a cigarette and no lighter might ask,

Have you fire?

- A second cause of mistakes is when learners think they know a rule, but in fact they don't know quite enough.

Thus, a learner who knows about the past tense -*ed* and who can say, 'I showed him the room', might also say,

He growed up in Canada.

This mistake would be caused by trying to use creatively what the learner already knows about English.

In another case, a learner might have made up a rule that is simply wrong in itself. Some students learn about making comparisons in English with -*er* and with *more* and they think that both have to be put together, in sentences such as,

Your room is more tidier than mine.

> Compared to standard English, these are mistakes. In their own minds, however, the students are successfully using their knowledge about the language.

- Thirdly, people may say things that they know are not correct, because this is still their best chance of getting their message across. This is another intelligent use of knowledge about English in order to communicate in English.

- Fourthly, mistakes can happen because someone is in a hurry, or tired, or thinking about something else. The exact details of which mistakes are made by native speakers and which are made by learners will often be different, but slips of the tongue or of the pen are found in everyone's English.

It is quite easy to think of possible causes of mistakes that learners make when speaking a foreign language, but it is very difficult indeed to say in any one case exactly what caused a particular mistake to occur. If we look at the categories we have outlined above, it is easy to imagine a student being affected by several things at once. That is to say, the student might be in a hurry, influenced by the words and structures of his or her first language, and also trying to apply a rule of English which may not be correct.

A teacher's view

It is very useful to have an idea about the possible causes of mistakes. What teachers need to know most about, however, is their learners. In this book, we shall divide up mistakes into different categories according to the teacher's opinion of how a mistake fits in with an individual student's stage of learning in his or her class.

Slips, errors and attempts

Slips

First of all, look at the following tiny mistakes of linguistic form. What do you think these mistakes have in common from the point of view of the learner?

He had been their for several days.
She left school two years ago and now work in a factory.
My father was a farmer. he wanted me to be a doctor.

My guess is that anyone who writes sentences such as these could correct the mistakes in them if they were pointed out. Teachers often call these 'careless mistakes' for just this reason. We know that if students concentrated their attention on these details, they could easily put them right.

So, whatever the cause of the mistakes, we can classify mistakes according to whether or not the teacher thinks that the student could correct them if given the chance.

If the teacher thinks that a student could self-correct a mistake, we shall call this type of mistake a **slip**.

Errors

Secondly, then, we must have a category for mistakes which individual students couldn't correct even if they were pointed out. Such mistakes will be different for different students, of course, or for the same student on different days, but the following were examples for some students:

Although the people are very nice, but I don't like it here.
That was the first English film which I have understood it.
It is fortunate the fact that she loves you.

With mistakes such as these, it is more difficult for the teacher to guess whether or not the student will be able to self-correct, although as teachers we probably think we can recognise what the student wanted to produce here and we may know that they have some familiarity with the correct forms.

> If a student cannot self-correct a mistake in his or her own English, but the teacher thinks that the class is familiar with the correct form, we shall call that sort of mistake an **error**.

Attempts

We can make one more distinction in this area of mistakes. Let's say we have a class of students who have not learnt much English, but they have learnt simple present and simple past tenses. If such a student says,

I wish I went my grandmother's house last summer.

then that student is trying to mean something but has no real idea of how to structure that meaning correctly in English. There is no point in talking about slips or errors here. In this example, the student has succeeded very well in communicating the meaning, but this is not always so. Take, for example, the following statement from a beginner,

This, no, really, for always my time. . . and then I happy.

There is no point in talking about slips or errors here, either. It is more useful to think of such mistakes as **attempts**.

> When the teacher knows that the students have not yet learned the language necessary to express what they want to say, we can call their mistakes **attempts**.
>
> When it is not clear what the students want to mean, or what structure they are trying to use, we can also call these mistakes **attempts**.

The distinctions we have suggested here describe mistakes from the point of view of learners and teachers. Teachers have to depend on their knowledge of their learners in order to decide how to categorise mistakes as they occur.

So, the mistake above,

I wish I went my grandmother's house last summer.

could be a slip for one student, an error for another, and an attempt for a third. Or, for the same learner, it might be an attempt today, an error next month, and a slip next year.

Now that we have these three categories of mistake to think about, we are one step closer to deciding what to do about them. In order to link ways of correction to mistakes, however, we have to give some thought to the significance of mistakes. That is what we do in the next chapter.

Summary

1 Mistakes of linguistic form can be caused by the influence of the first language, by misunderstanding a rule, by a decision to communicate as best one can, by lack of concentration, and by a mixture of those and other factors.

2 We can divide linguistic mistakes, according to the teacher's knowledge of his or her learners, into:
   - **slips**, which a student can self-correct;
   - **errors**, which a student can't self-correct, but where it is clear which form the student wanted to use, and where the class is familiar with that form;
   - **attempts**, where students have no real idea how to structure what they want to mean, or where intended meaning and structure are not clear to the teacher.

3 This division has to be made repeatedly by teachers, based on their knowledge of individual learners and classes.

Questions and activities

1 From your own situation, list some examples of first language influence on English pronunciation, vocabulary, grammar, ways of joining ideas together, and idiom.

2 Take some mistakes written by learners in your situation. What do you think caused these mistakes?

3 Using the same learner mistakes, do you think the writers will be able to self-correct? Discuss and then check with the learners to see if you were right.

4 Write down at least three sentences expressing your feelings about mistakes in language. Each sentence must contain the word 'mistake'. Here are some examples that were written by English language teachers:

My students make a lot of mistakes when they write.
I always correct mistakes as soon as they are made.
My students don't like to make mistakes.

Please write three or more sentences of your own.

When you have written the sentences, think about them again and see if it would make any difference if you used the word 'slip', 'error' or 'attempt' instead of 'mistake'. In other words, did you want to say something general about mistakes, or did your comment apply more to one kind of mistake than another?

The importance of mistakes

If you did Activity 4 at the end of Chapter 2, please look again at the sentences that you wrote there. If you didn't do that activity, please do the following one now.

> Think about the mistakes that your students make, or the mistakes you make yourself when using a language that's not your mother tongue. How do you feel about these mistakes? Please write down on a piece of paper at least three sentences expressing your experience of and feelings about mistakes in language. Each sentence must contain the word 'mistake'.

No, I mean it. Even if you've just sat down for a read, please do spend a few minutes thinking about this and write some sentences before you continue. Let me give you some examples that were written by English language teachers in the summer of 1987.

1 My students make a lot of mistakes when they write.
2 I always correct mistakes as soon as they are made.
3 My students don't like to make mistakes.

Please write three or more sentences of your own.

We usually think of mistakes as a problem. At the beginning of this book, however, we agreed that making mistakes is a part of learning. In the same way, the linguistic mistakes our students make are an important and necessary part of their language learning.

Learning steps

When a child is learning English as its mother tongue, there comes a stage when it says things such as:

Nina catched a balloon. or Nina got two foots.

What is happening here? The child has learned a rule for making a past tense and a rule for making plurals. In time, the child will learn that these two very good and useful rules also have exceptions to them. But at its present stage, the above statements are signs that the child is learning the language system. They are clear signals that learning steps are being made. It would be a very strange parent who wasn't pleased about these learning steps, who saw them as evidence of failure because they were mistakes! Now, there are certainly many differences between a child learning its mother tongue and our students in our classrooms. On the other hand, there are also some similarities, and this question of learning steps is one of them.

In the last chapter, we talked about mistakes by comparing what our students produce with the forms of standard English. Looked at in this way, mistakes seem like problems.

> But many of the things we call mistakes and see as problems are in fact signals that our students are successfully learning the language. They are taking the necessary learning steps.

Let's go back to the three sample sentences about mistakes that I gave you. I'm going to cross out the word 'mistakes', and write in 'learning steps'. The three examples now look like this:

learning steps
4 My students make a lot of ~~mistakes~~ when they write.

learning steps
5 I always correct ~~mistakes~~ as soon as they are made.

learning steps
6 My students don't like to make ~~mistakes.~~

In each case, we get a completely different picture of what is happening in our classrooms. Let's think about them separately.

In 4, we get the idea of students learning while they write, with each sentence that they write helping them in their language learning. So, if we take a sentence such as:

a) Although he is my friend, but I don't trust him.

we can say that there is a mistake in it. But if we compare it to an earlier sentence written by the same student:

b) Yes, is very beautiful, but I no like it here.

we can see that this student has made some learning steps. What we also have to remember is that writing sentence b) was a step on the way to writing sentence a).

The important thing is that we should not see a student's language only as something to be compared with correct standard English; we should see it as something developing in the student.

> Our job as teachers is not just to point out differences between our students' language and standard English. That is too negative a role. Our job is also to encourage the growth of the language by appreciating the learning steps.

Discouraging learning steps

Unfortunately, our good intentions sometimes work against us. Let's look again at sentence 5:

learning steps
I always correct ~~mistakes~~ as soon as they are made.

Of course, the teacher who wrote this wanted to be as helpful as possible to her students, but now we see a very real danger. Her students know that what they say will always be compared to standard English and that the teacher will always correct them when she spots any difference. So, they are careful not to say anything unless they are sure it is correct. That means that they will have very little opportunity to experiment with the language and to work out new and better ways of saying things. If they don't get lots of opportunity to make mistakes, they will have little chance to work out better rules.

Risks and chances

We can follow up the last idea by looking at sentence 6:

learning steps
My students don't like to make ~~mistakes.~~

Sentence 3 sounded very positive, how great to have students who don't like to make mistakes! But sentence 6 sounds terrible. If we have a class of students who don't like to make mistakes, that might mean that they don't take many learning steps, either. Imagine a teacher asking a class:

Teacher: Who knows someone who is a mechanic?
Eduard: Aaaah . . . my friend is a mechanic.
Teacher: OK, can you tell us the names of any of the tools your friend uses?

What Eduard really wanted to say was that his *brother-in-law* is a mechanic. But just as he started to speak, he realised that he didn't know the word, brother-in-law. Now he might have said:

Eduard: The man who married with my sister is a mechanic.

Or he might have said:

Eduard: My sister-husband is a mechanic.

But he didn't say either of these things, because he didn't want to risk making a mistake. So, we have two outcomes here:

• First, the student didn't learn how best to say what he really wanted to say, either for this time or for the future, because the teacher had no chance to help.
• Second, the idea was reinforced that it is best not to take any chances: no mistakes and no learning steps.

Where does this attitude come from? Partly, it depends on the learner: some people like to take chances and some don't. But to a very large extent, it depends on the teacher. Students quickly realise what teachers want and they usually try to supply it.

> If the teacher wants accuracy above all things and never mind what ideas the students express, then that teacher will get attempts at accuracy: no mistakes and no learning steps.

A change of heart

In the treatment of student language, we have to change our attitude towards mistakes. We must not think of them as something negative which needs some kind of punishment.

> Think of correction as a way of giving information, or feedback, to your students, just when it will support their learning.

So far, we have concentrated on mistakes and we have raised questions of correction. From now on, we shall concentrate on correction with reference back to what we have said about mistakes.

Summary

1 A lot of the things that we call mistakes can also be seen as learning steps. We should be pleased to see them.

2 Students should be encouraged to experiment with language so that they can take more learning steps.

3 Unless students make mistakes, they can't work out better rules for how to express what they want to say.

4 Correction must aim to support learners by giving feedback.

Questions and activities

1 Please look at the sentences that you wrote about mistakes. Cross out 'mistakes' and write in 'learning steps'. Now see what they make you think about mistakes and your attitude towards them.

2 If possible, discuss your ideas and reactions with a colleague who has also done the above activity.

Correction, fluency and accuracy

The most important decision regarding correction has to be made over and over again: to correct or not to correct?

Fluency

We can only talk about correction if we connect it with what we believe about teaching. It is not the teacher's job to correct all the non-standard English that learners produce. It is the teacher's job to help the learners improve their English, and sometimes this is best done by not correcting.

> When should we not correct our students?
> When we are paying attention to what they want to say.

The more attention we pay to what we want to say, the less we pay to correctness. If we pay too much attention to correctness, we don't seem to be speaking a language at all.

Let us look at two examples of this. Imagine two people who work together in a shop or an office. One morning one of them arrives late for work. What might be the next line in this conversation between them?

A: Why are you so late?
B: I'm sorry, my mother is take to hospital.
A: . . .

Now imagine the same conversation in a classroom if a student arrives late. We might hear:

Teacher: Why are you so late?
Student: I'm sorry, my mother is take to hospital.
Teacher: No, not "is take", she "has been taken" to hospital.

or:

Teacher: Why are you so late?
Student: I'm sorry, my mother has been taken to hospital.
Teacher: Good!

Well, that might be a slight exaggeration of what happens, but so often teachers do react to the form of what students say instead of to the content. Learning a language means more than learning lots of bits of linguistic form, and the only way to learn to communicate in a language is actually to communicate in that language.

Now imagine a class about to read a passage about volcanos. The teacher asks,

Has anyone ever seen a volcano? Ah, you have Tlapie.
Can you tell us something about it?

The teacher's aim here is to make a connection between the students' lives and what they are going to read. The teacher believes that this will make the passage more interesting and make it easier to understand. Which is the better answer?

Tlapie: It was very big.
Teacher: Right. Anyone else? Yes, Kyoko?
Kyoko: Yes, have see volcano. I' was las' year. I visi' aunt near coast. There was — don know how you call in Enrish — tsunami, very big wave. There is big volcano under sea. Make very big seas, Ver' excitin'.
Teacher: Goodness me! I wish I'd seen that! Thank you, Kyoko.

We should encourage answers like Kyoko's. At this point, we must show students that we are interested in what they have to say, and get them interested in the topic. Of course, we can make a mental note of mistakes that Kyoko makes in order to keep ourselves informed of how she is getting on, but if we now start to correct linguistic mistakes in what she says, we will get in the way of her learning.

This is a situation where the whole is much more than the sum of the parts. If we make Kyoko concentrate on the separate parts of what she wanted to say, we will make her communication much less efficient. Worse than that, we may take away her desire to communicate, and with it her chance of learning.

> There should always be times in our lessons when we simply encourage fluency. At such times, we don't correct linguistic mistakes unless they affect the communication of what the students want to say.

We must make sure that the students realise this, because it will make a clear difference to their ability and willingness to express themselves.

> In other words, the importance of mistakes is that they should often be ignored. Students need the experience of being listened to as people with things to say.

Accuracy

Of course, we cannot always ignore our students' correctness in their use of English. This is important because successful communication depends on a certain level of accuracy. It is also important because a lot of examinations are based on how accurate a student is in constructing correct pieces of language. The teacher's task is to help students progress through fluency towards the accuracy that they will need in order to get the education and the jobs they want.

So, there need to be times in our lessons when we focus our learners' attention on accuracy. Here, when we do decide to correct, we have to be sure that we are using correction positively to support learning.

> Correction is a way of reminding students of the forms of standard English. It should not be a kind of criticism or punishment.

Ask the students

It can be very useful to ask students how they feel about being corrected. At first, you will usually get whatever answer they think you want. But this question of correction is an interesting one for learners and teachers to discuss, because it is a part of the everyday experience that they share. As learners come to realise that there is a real question of choice involved, they will be encouraged to think about their own performance and their own feelings and preferences.

Through such discussion you are likely to discover something about how the students think they learn, and they are likely to discover something about how you think they learn.

The next three chapters deal with ways of correcting, starting from an emphasis on accuracy and moving towards fluency. The techniques of correction described in the following chapters have been found useful by many teachers in different situations, but please remember:

- Any technique can be improved by a certain teacher for a certain group of learners.
- No teaching technique is as important as the learners' feeling that the teacher is trying to help them learn. Techniques alone cannot give this feeling.

Summary

1 We need to balance fluency work, without correction, with accuracy work, where we use correction positively.

2 By reacting to what students say, as we would do with anyone else, we can encourage students to experience English as a real language.

3 It is useful to discuss correction with the students.

Questions and activities

1 When you learned a foreign language, were you given time to speak fluently without correction? If so, did you find it useful? If not, do you think it would have helped you?

2 What problems might be caused by not correcting?

3 Can you think of a time when one of your students tried to say something really interesting and original in English, as Kyoko did in the example on page 19?
a) What did he or she say, and how did you react?
b) If your students have never tried to say something like this, can you think of an explanation as to why they have not tried to do so?

4 Can teachers and students usefully discuss learning and teaching? Might this cause problems? What problems?

5 Is there a teaching idea that you have already changed to suit yourself or a certain class better? Have you seen an idea that you might change?

6 What kind of teacher behaviour could give the students the feeling that the teacher is interested in helping them?

Correction and accuracy in spoken English

When is correctness in spoken English most important for students in the language classroom? Most teachers would agree that spoken accuracy is most important for our learners when they are practising carefully something that has just been presented to them, such as a new verb tense, for example, or a way of comparing things.

Correcting the grammar

Imagine learners doing this exercise in class:

Example 1

Complete – World Records

Example: Greenland is the (large) island in the world.
  Greenland is the largest island in the world.

1. The (wide) street in the world is in Brasilia.
2. Mandarin is the (common) spoken language.
3. Many people think English food is the (bad) in the world.
4. The world's (valuable) painting is the Mona Lisa—La Gioconda.
5. The (dry) place in the world is the Atacama Desert in Chile.
6. The (hot) place in the world is Dallol in Ethiopia.
7. The (expensive) film ever made was '*War and Peace*'.
8. The (big) country in the world is the Soviet Union.
9. The (large) ocean is the Pacific.
10. The people of the USA smoke the (many) cigarettes.

After a student has said a sentence, the teacher leaves a few seconds pause so that all the students can decide whether the sentence was correct or not. If the sentence is correct, the teacher asks another student to do another sentence.

Some teachers like to say, 'Good!' when a student gets something right. Some teachers think that they shouldn't be involved in praise or criticism of the students. This is a personal decision for you to make, based on your knowledge of your students. What is important is that students feel that the teacher cares about their progress.

But what if the student makes a mistake? What does the teacher do then? The first thing to remember is that the best form of correction is **self-correction**.

Self-correction

People usually prefer to put their own mistakes right rather than be corrected by someone else. Also, self-correction is easier to remember, because someone has put something right in his or her own head. It is particularly important to give a chance for self-correction when you think that a mistake is what we have called a *slip*. So:

> Don't correct the mistake yourself, but show that a mistake has been made.

You can do this by the expression on your face, or by making a sign with your hand, or by saying something such as, 'Er....,' or 'Mmmm,' or whatever comes naturally.

> Then give the student a little time to recognise the mistake and correct it.

So, Example 1, above, might sound something like this:

Teacher:	Number 6,... Wu?
Wu:	The hottest place in the world is Dallol.
(pause)	
Teacher:	Right, Number 4,... Tay?
Tay:	The world's valuablest painting is The Mona Lisa.
(pause)	

Teacher:	Mmmmmmm (questioning expression on face)
(pause)	
Tay:	The world's most valuable painting is the Mona Lisa — La Giaconda.
(pause)	
Teacher:	Yes, good. Number 3, . . . Lee?

What if the student can't self-correct? The student may not know what to say, or may make another mistake. In this case, the teacher can ask if anyone else in the class can do this example correctly. This is called peer correction.

Peer correction

Peer correction is particularly useful in the case of what we called *errors*. Let's look at an example, in an exercise where the students are practising asking questions in the past simple tense.

Example 2

What time	go to bed last might?
	get up this morning?
	have breakfast today?
	leave home this morning?
	arrive at school?

The teacher asks one student to start by asking any one of the questions above. The student who answers asks another question, and so on:

Student 1:	What time did you have breakfast today, Rosa?
Rosa:	Half past seven.
	What time did you go to bed last night, Carmen?
Carmen:	Eleven o'clock.
	What time you arrive at school this morning, Luis?
Teacher:	(turns head as if didn't quite hear properly)
(pause)	
Carmen:	. . . Aah . . . What time, ah, you come to school?
(pause)	
Teacher:	Can anyone help? . . . Yes, Fernando?
Fernando:	What time did you arrive at school?
(pause)	
Teacher:	Yes, Carmen?
Carmen:	Ah, yes, What time did you arrive at school, Luis?

Notice that after peer correction, the teacher goes back to the student who made the mistake and gets her to ask the question again correctly.

Let's look more carefully at this idea of peer correction. It has certain advantages, but may also cause some problems.

Four advantages of peer correction

- Firstly, when a learner makes a mistake and another learner corrects it, both learners are involved in listening to and thinking about the language.
- Secondly, when a teacher encourages learners to correct each other's mistakes, the teacher gets a lot of important information about the students' ability. Can they hear a particular mistake? Can they correct it?
- Thirdly, the students become used to the idea that they can learn from each other. So, peer correction helps learners cooperate and helps make them less dependent on teachers.
- Fourthly, if students get used to the idea of peer correction without hurting each other's feelings, they will be able to help each other learn when they work in pairs and groups, when the teacher can't hear what is said.

Two problems with peer correction

- Firstly, when the teacher asks for peer correction from the whole class, it might be that the same two or three people always want to answer.

If this is the case, teachers need to call on other students who do not volunteer, or to give more help with the correction themselves. It is not good for the class if the same few students do the correction all the time. The idea of peer correction is to encourage cooperation, not to put one or two students in the traditional place of the teacher.

- Secondly, if students are not used to correcting each other, they may find it very difficult to change their habits.

They may just listen negatively for mistakes. They may feel that they are being criticised by people who have no right to criticise them. They may feel that the teacher is not doing his or her job properly. In this sort of atmosphere, peer correction is useless if not damaging.

So, if you live in a country where your students are used to working as separate individuals and where they feel they can only learn or accept correction from the teacher, you have a difficult decision to make. Either you don't use peer correction because it is unfamiliar to your students, or you slowly introduce peer correction so that they can get used to it, at first in controlled situations such as the one above. This is another area in which discussion between teacher and students can be very useful, because students need to understand the purpose of what they are being asked to do.

Teacher correction

If we think that a mistake needs to be corrected, and if neither the student who made the mistake, nor any other student can correct it, then the teacher has to give more help. This still doesn't mean that the teacher has to give the correct form straight away.

> The more the students are involved in correction, the more they have to think about the language used in the classroom.

So, if self-correction and peer correction fail at first, the teacher can sometimes help by focusing attention on the place where the mistake occurs. In the following exercise, the students are practising the passive:

Example 3

Make sentences

1863 The London Underground opened
The London Underground was opened in 1863.

1826 The first photgraph taken
1879 The electric light bulb invented
1885 The motor cycle invented
1928 Penicillin discovered
1945 The atom bomb first used
1953 Mount Everest first climbed
1960 John Kennedy elected President of USA
1968 Martin Luther King killed

Teacher:	1928,...Ali?
Ali:	Penicillin was discovered in 1928.
(pause)	
Teacher:	Yes, 1885,...Khalid?
Khalid:	The motor cycle was invent in 1885.
(pause)	
Teacher:	Well,...
(pause)	
Khalid:	The motor cycle...
(pause)	
Teacher:	Anybody?
(pause)	
Teacher:	The motor cycle was... in..vent..?

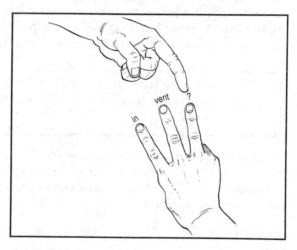

As the teacher says, 'in...vent...,' she holds up three
fingers of one hand to show that the word has three syllables in it.
She points to the first finger as she says, 'in' and the second finger
as she says, 'vent'. As she points to the third finger, she pauses and
looks questioningly at the class, hoping that someone will add the
'ed'. If someone does, she asks for the whole word and then the
whole sentence before returning to Khalid.

This technique of counting on fingers can be used whenever
something is missing, whether it is a sound, or a syllable in a word,
or a word in a sentence. It is best for a teacher to count from right
to left, because this looks like left to right for the students facing
the teacher.

At the same time, it is important to remember that gestures can mean different things in different societies. Teachers must be careful not to do anything which might seem impolite to the learners they are working with.

Two other ways of pointing out the mistake in Khalid's answer above would be to:
- repeat the sentence up to the mistake and then invite someone to continue: 'The motorcycle was...'
- repeat the sentence including the mistake, show by your face and your voice where the mistake is, and then ask for correction: 'The motorcycle was...invent (?)...in 1885.'

As a last resort, if all other possibilities fail, the teacher gives the correct form and then says the whole sentence. As no one has been able to make the correction, the teacher will often ask the whole class to repeat the correct sentence together before asking Khalid to say it.

There are two more points to note here:
- When a teacher finds that no one in a class can correct a particular mistake, the teacher must realise that this point has not yet been generally learned. Even though the teacher might think that he or she has taught it, it obviously needs teaching again in a different way.

- When correcting a mistake such as the one above, there is a danger of overstressing the corrected part in order to make the correction clear. Here, it might sound like:

Teacher: InvenTED. The motor cycle was inventIED in 1885.

This is obviously something to avoid, otherwise we are teaching mistakes of form rather than correcting them. We must keep to natural stress and pronunciation so that our students can actually hear what they are supposed to produce. Let us look at this in more detail.

Correcting the saying

So far, we have looked at exercises which are used for practising the accurate saying of particular structures. In these exercises, we have concentrated on mistakes in the major grammatical point of the exercise.

When the exercises are being spoken, however, the teacher should encourage students to sound as though they are saying something which makes sense, not merely speaking a list of words from a page. As far as spoken English is concerned, saying:

The — widest — street — in — the — world — is — in — Brasilia.

in an expressionless voice is also not very correct. The teacher should at least decide where the stressed syllables are in the sentence and show this to the students by tapping on a desk, or clapping, or by beating the air with a hand:

The WIDest street in the WORLD is in BraSILia.

When a student gets a sentence grammatically correct, but sounds lifeless, the teacher should ask for a more natural saying of the sentence. Some students feel embarrassed about this at first, so a good way to begin is by having all the students say the sentence together.

Intonation is equally important. We can't teach intonation on its own, it has to be a part of what is said. When a student says something without any real intonation, it isn't really correct. As we saw in Chapter 1, sounding polite is often more important than being grammatically correct. And politeness is very closely tied to intonation.

So, even when you are doing exercises such as the ones we have been looking at here, try to get the students to speak with suitable intonation. This becomes even more important in exercises such as the following, partly because question intonation is often difficult for learners, and partly because requests such as these certainly need to sound polite. Teachers should give a lively model themselves and encourage students who say sentences meaningfully:

Example 4

Asking permission to borrow things

Do you think I could borrow your car?
Yes, as long as I can have it back tomorrow.

Do you think you could lend me your car?
Yes, as long as I can have it back tomorrow.

| 1. road map | 3. scarf | 5. £1 |
| 2. dictionary | 4. umbrella | 6. bike |

Another good way to help is to write part of the sentence on the board, underline the word with the loudest stress, and show with a line whether the voice goes up or down from there.

...borrow your <u>car?</u>

...lend me your <u>umbrella?</u>

We can make a general point about stress and intonation:

> We can help students improve their stress and intonation if we give them something to see as well as something to hear.

There is one obvious difficulty here: if the students are reading a sentence out of a book, how can they watch the teacher's hands or look up at the board? There is a simple answer to this question, which also helps us in the use of dialogues:

> Students should not read out each sentence from the page. Tell them to read the sentence silently, then look up and say it.

In this way, the students are a litle closer to practising reading and speaking, and they can take advantage of visual help with their pronunciation. This approach will also let the teacher know if the students are ready to say what they are trying to say. There is little use in students reading out one word after another without knowing how they fit together to make sense.

Although stress and intonation are more important, the pronunciation of individual sounds in words is also worth correcting when you notice that an obvious mistake occurs frequently. Let's take another response from example 3 above.

Teacher: 1953, ...Mansour?
Mansour: Mount Everest was first clime/bed in 1953.
Teacher: Yes, but...

In other words, Mansour pronounces the /b/ in *climbed* and says the word as two syllables. As Mansour has produced the structure correctly, the teacher decides that it is worth correcting the pronunciation. Having shown that the main point was correct, but that something is wrong, the teacher now wants to focus Mansour's attention on the problem. She holds up her hand and counts the words on her fingers from right to left as she speaks, one finger for each word:

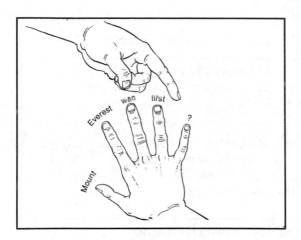

Teacher: Mount Everest was first . . . ?
Mansour: Clime/bed.

The teacher shakes her head. Mansour now knows where the problem is. The teacher repeats the sentence. This time, when she gets to the verb, she holds up two fingers and squeezes them together to show that Mansour is making two syllables where there should be one:

Teacher: Mount Everest was first . . .
Mansour: Climbed.
Teacher: Right, Mount . . . ?
Mansour: Mount Everest was
               first climbed in 1953.
Teacher: Good.

Perhaps Mansour is still saying the /b/ in *climbed*, but the teacher has made the more important correction and may well think that that is enough for now. We don't want to correct people so much that they lose their enthusiasm for what they are learning. On another occasion, the teacher may simply write a letter b on the board and cross it out as a clue to the correct pronunciation: ̶b̶

> Correction should not mean insisting on everything being absolutely correct. Correction means helping students to become more accurate in their use of language.

So far in this chapter, we have looked at the kind of spoken exercise that learners often do when they have just learned something in class. Many teachers use dialogues to present and practise new material, and these give a good opportunity for working on stress and intonation. So, let's put together some of the points that we have mentioned for use with a dialogue.

Dialogues

The first thing to say about correction here is that you should let the student get to the end of what he or she is supposed to be saying. Don't interrupt. If it's a short dialogue, let the students finish the whole dialogue before you give feedback.
Hearing one's own mistakes in stress and intonation is very difficult, but peer correction can work if another student can give a model of how something should be said:

Sow Ling:	Good morning.
Angel:	Good morning. I need a ballpoint pen.
Sow Ling:	Yes, sir. What colour?
Angel:	A blue ONE, please.
Sow Ling:	Here you are. That's just a dollar. Thank you.
Angel:	Thank you. Bye.
Sow Ling:	Goodbye.
Teacher:	Fine. What did you say when she asked you about the colour?
Angel:	A blue ONE, please.
Teacher:	Yes, I don't think that sounds quite right. Anybody?
Gudrun:	Maybe we should say: "A BLUE one, please."
Teacher:	Yes, I think so. You can have a BLUE one, or a RED one, or a BLACK one. You are choosing the COLOUR, so you stress the COLOUR. Angel, what COLOUR would you like?
Angel:	A BLACK one, please.
Teacher:	Good. OK, who's next?

In this piece of correction, the teacher is doing lots of things. She uses peer correction to provide a correct model for Angel to listen to. Then, she also adds a little explanation of why one particular word is stressed. This will help some students notice the different stress and understand the sense behind it. Then she goes back to Angel to ask him to say the line again.

Every time the teacher stresses a word here: *BLUE, RED, BLACK, COLOUR*, she taps her finger on the desk, or quietly claps her hands together, or nods her head. In other words, she does something that the students can see in order to support the stress that she wants them to hear. She could do this for the sentence that is causing the problem by using her fingers in the way we have talked about before. If there is no peer correction at the end of the dialogue, the teacher says:

Teacher:	OK, listen. Sow Ling asks you what colour you want and you say: (Teacher holds up four fingers and taps them one by one as Angel speaks.)
Angel:	A blue ONE, please.
Teacher:	(Taps the four fingers again, but tapping harder and for longer on the second finger. She does this twice.)
Angel:	A BLUE one, please.
Teacher:	Right!

In the case of intonation, the teacher can draw lines in the air with a hand, or draw lines on the board to show the voice moving up or down in parts of the dialogue where the students make mistakes:

A blue one, please.

In the next chapter, we shall look at correction in less controlled language work, but first let's look again at the most important points we've made in this chapter on careful practice.

Summary

1 Give a chance for self-correction and, if possible, use peer correction rather than direct teacher correction.

2 However the correction is done, ask the student who first made the mistake to repeat the correct utterance.

3 Concentrate on the most important learning points.

4 In spoken practice, work on the correctness of stress and intonation, using visual support.

5 Correction should mean helping people become more accurate, not insisting on completely standard English.

6 Involving learners in making judgements about correctness helps them become more accurate in their own use of the language.

Questions and activities

1 Did your teachers give you time to correct yourself, or use peer correction? How did you feel about it?

2 Have you already used these forms of correction as a teacher? How do you feel about them?

3 How do/would students in your teaching situation feel about peer correction?

4 Are there other techniques in this chapter that you have already used? How do you feel about them?

5 Are there any techniques in this chapter that you can't imagine using? Why?

6 What techniques do you use that you think should be in a chapter like this?

7 When discussing Example 3, we talked about the danger of teaching a wrong stress when correcting (see page 29). Can you see a similar danger when correcting the example on page 25?

8 Find an exercise that you will have to teach. Then write down some common mistakes that you would expect learners to make. Discuss these with some colleagues and ask them to make the agreed mistakes while you take them through the exercise. Practise encouraging self-correction and peer correction.

9 Try out a technique that you haven't used before with a class and discuss what happens.

References

The examples from textbooks in this chapter are taken from:

Example 1 *Encounters* by J. Garton-Sprenger, T.C. Jupp, J. Milne and P. Prowse, p 125 (Heinemann 1979)

Example 3 *Exchanges* by P. Prowse, J. Garton-Sprenger and T.C. Jupp, p 40 (Heinemann 1981)

Example 4 *Studying Strategies* by B. Abbs and I. Freebairn, p 37 (Longman 1982)

Correction and fluency in spoken English

If students spend all their time doing careful practice of separate pieces of language, they will not learn to use the language in real situations. When students are trying to use the language, the kind of correction that we looked at in the last chapter is harmful to learning. We discussed the reasons for this in Chapters 3 and 4, but we can say here very briefly that:

- Students need the experience of uninterrupted, meaningful communication if they are to learn to use the language.
- If students are to say anything meaningful, they need to feel that people are listening to *what* they are saying, not to *how* they are saying it.
- Making mistakes in language use is not only normal, but necessary to language learning.

For some of the time, then, it is important that students are not corrected, but simply encouraged. However, between the techniques of the last chapter and the total lack of any form of correction, there are other techniques which teachers can use. They are the subject of this chapter.

Delayed correction

Exercises

After going through an exercise with the whole class, teachers will often want to increase the amount of practice for learners by getting them to do an exercise in pairs. In the following exercise, for instance, pairs of students take turns to make an offer, promise or decision, while the partner makes an appropriate response, such as, '*Thanks,*' or '*OK*'. So, in a class of forty, there would be twenty pairs doing the exercise at the same time, while the teacher walks round and listens:

Example 1

Make offers, promises or decisions

Examples: A friend hasn't any money. Offer to lend him
some.
I'll lend you some money.

A friend asks you to lock the door. Promise not
to forget.
I won't forget.

1. You are going to the theatre with a friend. Offer to book
the tickets.
2. You are ordering a meal in a restaurant. Decide to have
roast beef
3. The phone is ringing. Offer to answer it.
4. You are saying goodbye to a friend. Promise to write to
him.
5. A tourist is looking for the post office. Offer to show him
the way.
6. It is difficult to park in the city. Decide not to take the
car.
7. You've got toothache. Decide to go to the dentist
tomorrow.
8. You are meeting a friend at the station. Promise not to
be late.

What happens if someone makes a mistake? Teachers can't even
hear most of the students, and if they stop to correct someone,
they'll certainly miss lots more mistakes.

Don't worry! This is a difficult stage for many teachers,
but we have to leave the students alone so that they
can get on with some learning.

This is a good place to start giving the students a little freedom,
because the examples with the exercise mean that all the students
should know exactly what they have to do.

The teacher walks round the class quickly to make sure
that all the students are working properly.

She only stops if she finds that some students don't know what to do, or are doing the wrong things. If this is true of lots of pairs, the best idea is to stop the whole class and ask one pair to show everyone again what they are to do.

> When the teacher hears mistakes, she makes a note of them. This is important information for the teacher.

If she hears a mistake repeatedly, she can wait until the pairs have finished the exercise and then ask someone to do the question in which she heard the mistake.

In Example 1, imagine the teacher has heard some students say:

I go to the dentist tomorrow.

When the pairs have finished, she says,

Teacher: Right, can someone do number 7 for us again?
Yes, Hans and Jacques.
Hans: I'll go to the dentist tomorrow.
Jacques: Good idea.
(pause)
Teacher: Good. Could another pair do that one again?
Peter and Werner?
Peter: I go to the dentist tomorrow.

Teacher:	(questioning expression) Er . . . (pause) Not quite. Yes, Josef?
Josef:	I'll go . . .
Teacher:	Yes, can you hear that "ll" in there, Peter?
Peter:	Ach, so, I *will* go.
Teacher:	Mmm. I — will, I'll.

(As she says this, the teacher holds up two fingers. She points to one finger for "I" and the other finger for "will". Then she squeezes the two together for "I'll".)

Teacher:	So, Peter?
Peter:	I'll go to the dentist tomorrow.
Werner:	Bad luck!
Teacher:	Very good. Fine.

If the teacher hears lots of mistakes in important points she has been trying to teach, she need not think too much about correction. She must realise that the class has not understood what she has presented and she needs to think of different ways of presenting the same point again. Teachers can get this important information only if they give learners the chance to make mistakes.

Communication activities

As well as controlled exercises such as the last one, it is important that students do freer activities in pairs or small groups. Here is one example, where the class has been working together with the teacher, describing people in pictures:

Example 2

Practice

Look at everyone in the room very carefully for a couple of minutes. Then stand back to back with one of them and, *without looking*, describe each other. Keep going until everyone has had a turn.

As before, the teacher walks round the class and makes notes. This is a difficult and important part of a teacher's work. The teacher has to:

- decide if the class has learned well enough what was taught;
- notice what mistakes are made;
- decide if it is worth doing more work on these mistakes;
- decide how to do any necessary correction.

So, although it may not look as though teachers are 'teaching' at this stage of a lesson, they are working very hard in order to help the learners do their learning!

If there are common mistakes, the teacher can write them on the board after the activity and ask for correction from the class:

Teacher: I heard a few people saying these things.
           What's wrong with them?
           "She has about fourteen years."
           "I have seen her yesterday."

These mistaken forms can now be corrected by the whole class without anyone being interrupted. As students make their corrections, either the teacher or the students change the sentences on the board until they are correct.

She h̶a̶s̶ *is* about fourteen years ∧ *old*

I h̶a̶v̶e̶ ̶s̶e̶e̶n̶ *Saw* her yesterday.

While doing this type of correction, the teacher has a chance not only to correct mistakes, but also to explain what was wrong, or to have students give their explanations.

Explanation

A student might correct the second sentence above by saying:

"Have seen" is wrong. It should be "saw."

Or, a student might say:

The verb should be in the past simple, because it's "yesterday".

Which is better? Should the teacher explain, or ask for an explanation of the mistake? Here again, we find that questions about correction are at the centre of questions about teaching.

If you use explanation as part of your teaching, you can use it as part of your correction. It will help some students, but not all. The ability to talk about the language is certainly helpful to a lot of learners, but remember that it is being able to use English that is most important, not being able to explain it.

> Don't give long grammatical explanations yourself.
> Encourage the students to explain in their own way.

This can have three big advantages:
- The students find a need for words such as 'verb', 'tense', 'plural', etc. which will help them learn these useful terms.
- The teacher gets useful insights into just what the students do understand, and how they see the language.
- Teacher and students build together their own way of talking about the language.

Peer correction

We introduced the idea of peer correction in the last chapter. If students can get used to correcting each other in a positive way, this can be very helpful during pair and group work.

When students are working together on a sentence-by-sentence exercise, they can take turns to comment on each other's sentences. Let's look at another example. Notice, too, how these students have been encouraged to respond to their partner, even though this is only an exercise:

Example 3

IT'S GOOD OF YOU TO SHOW ME ROUND.

I'M GRATEFUL TO YOU FOR GIVING ME A LIFT.

Say thank you to these people:

Mark gave you a lift.
Martin and Jillian translated the letter for you.
Gloria did your shopping for you.
Eddy lent you a book.

Mike got you a taxi.
Cathy helped you wash up.
Tim let you stay in his house.
John carried your heavy suitcase.

Olga:	It's good of you to give me a lift.
Laura:	My pleasure.
	I am grateful for you for translating the letter.
Olga:	You're welcome, Er,. . .it's "grateful *to* you".
Laura:	What I say?
Olga:	"Grateful *for* you," I think.
Laura:	Oh. Well, I am grateful to you for translating the letter. And I'm grateful to you for correcting me!
Olga:	Not at all!

If the students aren't sure what is correct, they can make a note of their difficulty, carry on with the exercise, and ask the teacher later.

> What happens if the partner doesn't notice a mistake?
> The students continue with their work.

At this stage of learning, it is much more important that the students get lots of practice in the language than that everything is absolutely correct.

In fluency activities, we don't want the learners to be interrupting each other. They should concentrate on *what* their partner is saying. Occasionally, however, it is useful to have someone concentrating on how things are said. In addition to the teacher walking round the class and making notes, it is possible to turn some of the students into observers.

Observers

Take the following as an example of an activity where an observer might be useful:

Example 4

> Work in groups. Choose four jobs and
> decide which school subjects are
>
> ✓✓ necessary   ✓ useful   ✗ useless
>
> for each one

	Architect	Banker	Doctor	Engineer	Farmer	Journalist	Photographer	Secretary	Businessman or Businesswoman
Mathematics									
English									
Geography									
Latin									
History									
Typing									
Biology									
Art									
Physics									
Chemistry									

The students work in groups of four. Three of them carry out the
activity while the fourth one listens and tries to note down some
mistakes that the others make. This student is the observer. The
teacher makes sure that different students take turns at being the
observer.

When the activity is finished, the observer shows the others what
he or she has written down and the group discusses what is correct
and what is wrong. Disagreements can be referred to the teacher.

This use of an observer can be very profitable for learners, but the observer's job is very difficult and it is important for the teacher to make clear what this job is and what it is not:

- It is not the observer's job to try to catch every mistake.
- It is not the observer's job to correct the other students in the group.
- It is the observer's job to write down some things that might be incorrect, impolite, or otherwise wrong.
- It is the group's job to get on with the activity and not take any notice of the observer.
- It is then the group's job to discuss what the observer has written down and to decide what is correct.

Like so many changes in classroom practice, students will find this difficult at first. But once they get used to it, it becomes a normal part of an activity, with the following advantages:

- A fluency activity can be followed by a focus on the accuracy of what the students actually said. This puts communication first, but includes work on accuracy.
- The students are encouraged to make their own decisions about correctness. This gives them more responsibility for their use of language.
- Weaker students can also help stronger students by bringing to their attention mistakes that they make.
- The observer can reduce the amount of talk that goes on in the students' own language if they share one. One possible observer task is to write down anything that is said in the native language and, when the activity is over, the first group task is to decide how to say these things in English.

> Despite these positive points, however, the observer should not be used too often. Part of the experience of learning a language is using it without having someone listen to *how* you say things. This remains important.

We have now looked at ways of correcting language in exercises and freer activities. Finally, in this chapter, we look at what the teacher can do in normal conversation with learners.

Normal conversation

First of all, let us emphasise how important it is that learners get the chance to have some normal conversation with each other and with the teacher, outside exercises and activities. Obviously, the idea of correction is impossible in a conversation, but there are some things that a teacher can do to help give form to what is said.

- Firstly, the teacher can react normally to what students say in actual situations. For example:
  Rosa hasn't brought her homework to class. In her country, it is proper for her to apologise to the teacher and say why she hasn't brought the work. In some countries, perhaps this would not be appropriate, but it is a good idea to look for opportunities in the classroom where students can be encouraged to use English socially.

In this situation, we want Rosa to make her apology in English. If she does so, this should be accepted in the normal social way. She should not be congratulated if her English is grammatical, or corrected if it is not. If we judge her English in either way, we are denying her attempt to use English appropriately, and treating everything that she says as a linguistic exercise.

Both the following, then, are of equal value for Rosa:

Rosa: Am sorry. Have forget the book at home.
Teacher: Alright, Rosa. Please bring it tomorrow.

Rosa: I am very sorry. I'm afraid I've left my book at home.
Teacher: Alright, Rosa. Please bring it tomorrow.

- Secondly, things that we say in normal conversation are a natural way for a teacher to deal with student problems in speech. We often say such things as:

a) Sorry, I didn't catch that.

or

b) Really? Do you mean that. . .?

and these can be very useful for the language learner and teacher.

Expressions such as b) are particularly good. They are natural, they keep a conversation going, and they supply a correct form of what the speaker wanted to say both for the speaker and for anyone else who is listening. This technique of repeating something in a slightly different way can be used when you aren't sure of what the speaker means, or when it is quite clear; when someone makes a mistake, or when they are just searching for a word:

Subhi: Geography is a scholarship for the earth and the people.
Teacher: How do you mean? Like a relationship?
Subhi: Yes, yes. It make a relationship between the earth and the people.
Teacher: Yes, I see what you mean. That's a nice way of putting it.

Louise: Oui, I am going there all the Tuesdays.
Teacher: Oh, you go there every week, do you? You must like it!

Teacher: Who do you want to win the game?
Victoria: It is the same.
Teacher: Oh, you don't care? I am surprised!

Gülten: Have you. . .a. . .for. . .my pencil is break?
Teacher: A pencil sharpener? Sure, here you are.

Exchanges of this sort happen frequently in normal conversation between any users of English. It is important, of course, that the teacher says these things naturally, not like a correction. Learners need to feel that they are involved in a conversation in English, not another exercise.

Summary

1 The teacher needs to arrange pair and group work in a way that will suit the local situation.

2 The teacher makes sure that the students are working, but doesn't interrupt their work.

3 The teacher moves round the class and makes notes of important mistakes. These can be corrected with the whole class later.

4 When doing an exercise with separate items in it, students can try to correct each other.

5 When doing freer activities, one of the students can sometimes act as observer, to note mistakes for discussion.

6 When talking conversationally to students, the teacher can help by supplying words, or repeating something to make it clear, as long as this is done in a natural and relaxed way.

> Most importantly, the possibility of not correcting must always be at the front of the teacher's mind. In order to bring about fluency in language use, encouragement is more important than correction.

Questions and activities

1 What is your experience of group work, as learner or teacher?

2 Are there techniques in this chapter that you have already used? How do you feel about them?

3 Are there techniques in this chapter that you can't imagine using? Why?

4 What other techniques ought to be in this chapter?

5 Look at an activity that encourages communication. What mistakes would you expect your students to make?

6 With a group of colleagues, take turns to be the observer while others carry out an activity and make typical mistakes. Check which mistakes the observers write down.

7 Which of these mistakes would be worth doing extra work on?

8 Try out in class a technique you haven't used before and discuss what happens.

References

Example 1 *Encounters* by J. Garton Sprenger, T.C. Jupp, J. Milne and P. Prowse, p 124 (Heinemann 1979)

Example 2 *Functions of English* by L. Jones, p 75 (Cambridge University Press 1977)

Example 3 *Communicate 1* by K. Morrow and K. Johnson, p 89 (Cambridge University Press 1979)

Example 4 *Cambridge English Course* by M. Swan and C. Walter, p 123 (Cambridge University Press 1984)

Correction and writing

Many of the things that we said about the correction of spoken language are also true for the correction of written language. We can certainly keep in mind the last two points that we made in Chapter 5:

- Correction should mean helping people to become more accurate, not insisting on completely standard English.
- Involving learners in judgements about correctness helps them become more accurate in their own use of the language.

It is very depressing for a student to get back any piece of written work with lots of teacher correction on it. We know that students often just look at the mark they have been given, put the paper away and forget about it. By keeping the above two ideas about help and involvement in mind, perhaps we can improve this situation a little.

Self-correction and slips

Exercises

Let's begin again by looking at the correction of exercises. We shall concentrate on the major point of the exercise. For example:

Example 1

IT IS *ADJECTIVE + INFINITIVE*

Look at the following sentence from the text.

> *It is frightening to realise that a small test-tube full of germs could destroy a whole civilisation.* (Lines 15–17)

This is a combination of the following two sentences
 i) A small test-tube full of germs could destroy a whole civilisation.
 ii) When anyone realises this, it is frightening/Realising this is frightening.

1 Join the following pairs of sentences in the same way.
 a) Someone from our country has won a gold medal. It is exciting when anyone hears this.
 b) Some parents maltreat their children. Believing this is hard.
 c) A spider spins its web. When we see how this is done, it is fascinating.
 d) More and more young people are going to university. When anyone sees this, it is encouraging.
 e) One day people will be living on Venus. Visualising this is difficult.

If a student is getting the main point correct, we can mark smaller mistakes:

a) It is exciting to hear that someone from our country has won a gold medal.

b) It is hard to believe that some parents maltreat their children.

c) It is fascinating to see how a spider spin its web.

But if the student is making a mistake on the major point of the exercise, we should concentrate attention on this, not on other details:

d) It is exciting to hear that someone from our country has won a gold medal.

e) It is hard to believe that some parents maltreat their children.

f) It is fascinating to see that how a spider spin its web.

Notice that the teacher here has not corrected the mistake, but has pointed out that there is a mistake. Just as in spoken English, we first want to give the student a chance of self-correction.

For self-correction to work, we have to give a little time at the beginning of a lesson for students to look at their marked work and try to correct any mistakes. By using some lesson time in this way, we show the students that we think it is important for them to look through their work again and give some thought to what they wrote. For this reason also, it is important to give written work back to the learners as soon as possible after they have completed it.

In the case of the two examples given above, the teacher believes that self-correction will work. In the first case,

c)...a spider spin,

the teacher thinks that this mistake is just a *slip*. When the student's attention is concentrated on the mistake, he or she will correct it easily.

In the second case,

f)... It is fascinating to see that how,

the exercise itself, with its examples, provides lots of help for the student to work out the correct sentence now that he or she knows that the first attempt was wrong.

If a lot of students make the same mistake, the teacher knows that there is a general difficulty and that something has to be taught again in a different way.

Less controlled writing

In less controlled writing, the teacher can make self-correction easier in two ways:
- by marking only one particular kind of mistake, one which would be useful for a particular student, or,
- by giving the students some information about what kind of mistake they have made.

For example, if there is a spelling mistake, you can write S in the margin; if it is a mistake of word order, you write WO. Here is an example from one of my advanced students:

More than tow million pilgrims come to Mecca every year and   *S*
always we wonder how we can cope with them.   *WO*

The spelling mistake here is a very small one, but I want to point it out because this student makes it very often. I haven't underlined the mistake because I want the student to find it himself. I hope that making him concentrate in this way will help him stop making the mistake.

I have underlined the word order mistake, because I want to give the student more help with seeing where the mistake is. In this case, if I don't give that help, there is a danger that the student will start to doubt the word order of *how we can cope*, which is perfectly correct.

So, by underlining mistakes, or by giving clues in the margin, or by using both together, the teacher can help students see and correct mistakes in their own writing. These are some other signals that I have found useful:

$\mathcal{S}$	Spelling	WO	Word Order
$\mathcal{P}$	Punctuation	C	Connection of ideas
T	Tense	Ref	Reference in text
A	Article	$\wedge$	Something missing here
W	Wrong Word	C	Start a new paragraph

It doesn't matter exactly what signals you use, although it would help if all the English teachers in a school could agree on a set. The important thing is that your students understand what you mean by them, and that the signals help the students concentrate on mistakes in their writing that they can correct themselves.

In Chapter 2, we divided mistakes up into *slips, errors* and *attempts*. The kind of correction that we have looked at here is good for *slips*, because students can correct these mistakes when they have their attention focused on them and they also have time to think. But what about the mistakes we called *errors*, where the individual can't self-correct, but some members of the class probably can correct the mistakes in question? This is where peer correction can be very useful.

Peer correction and errors

The simplest way of doing peer correction is to proceed in the ways described above for self-correction, but to have students work together in pairs or groups. There are two great advantages to this:

- When two students work together on correcting each other's work, the discussion helps each one to learn from his or her own errors. Two heads are better than one.
- We all have difficulty in seeing our own mistakes, even if a teacher has given us a signal as to what sort of a mistake it is. Cooperation helps develop an ability to see our own mistakes.

Another way of using peer correction is to organise a correction group.

Correction groups

1 Divide your class up into four or five groups. If, for example, you have forty students in your class, you can divide your class into four groups of ten. The groups then take it in turns to be the correction group for a writing class.

2 While the rest of the class gets on with this week's writing task, the correction group is given last week's piece of work which the teacher has marked, as described above, but not corrected. This means that three quarters of your class do the new writing task each week.

3 Each student in the correction group, then, has his or her own paper and two others to look at. The students in the correction group work in twos or threes to correct the important mistakes that the teacher has marked.

4 For the last part of the lesson, the students from the correction group return the papers to the students who wrote them and explain the corrections that they have made. The teacher goes round the class and helps where there are any disagreements or questions.

All the comments that we made in the last chapter about the need for a feeling of cooperation if peer correction is to work are equally true here. There is, however, one great advantage to the teacher in encouraging the cooperative use of peer correction in written work:

> All these techniques reduce the amount of time that the teacher has to spend on correcting written work, while also increasing the usefulness of correction to the learner.

Whole class correction

The teacher can make a collection of mistakes from a class's writing and put them on the board for discussion. Obviously, you choose mistakes that you think it would be useful for the students to think about and correct. Make sure that you give the mistake in enough context, at least a sentence, so that the learners can see where something went wrong.

You can correct unimportant mistakes before you write up the examples in order to concentrate attention on what is important. It is also probably best to change any details which might give away which student has written any one mistake. This activity then allows the teacher to use actual student writing for class correction without embarrassing any individual student.

Another possibility is to mix in with the mistakes examples of student writing which you think are particularly good. In this way, students are being invited first to evaluate what they read rather than just look for mistakes. It also means that the teacher can make positive comments on the class's writing while giving useful models and encouragement.

You can sometimes turn the last activity into a competition.

Correction competitions

1 With forty students in the class, the teacher can put ten mistakes on the board, or ten sentences of which seven or eight contain mistakes.

2 The class is divided into ten groups of four.

3 The groups work to correct the sentences.

4 Then the teacher calls out one of the sentences on the board and asks one of the groups to say if something is wrong.

5 If so, they must say what is wrong, and what a suitable correction would be. For each of these steps, the group gets one point if they are right.

6 Other groups can challenge their answer and win points for themselves.

7 Eventually, the mistake is corrected on the board and the class moves on to another item and another group.

8 Finally, the points are counted to find the winning group.

It is easy to make up variations on the above game and on the way of scoring.

> The basic idea is to give the students some fun while they are concentrating on accuracy. At the same time, they are getting used to cooperating with fellow students to correct their own mistakes.

Let us now turn to the correction of *attempts* — where the student is trying to say something, but really doesn't know how to express that meaning, and when the teacher is not always sure what the learner was trying to say.

Teacher correction and attempts

Sometimes, the teacher can leave these parts alone and concentrate the student's attention on mistakes in the writing which the student can correct, and which will help the student's learning because the student is ready to learn that particular point. Remember, correction doesn't mean making everything absolutely correct; correction means helping people learn to express themselves better.

Sometimes, however, the student's *attempts* are an important part of what the student is trying to mean, and then the teacher should not ignore them. In these cases, it's usually too complicated to try to change or underline bits of what the student has written. The teacher can provide a correct way of writing what he or she thinks the student wanted to write, and ask if this is what the student meant. Here, I use a big question mark as a signal:

Later he thought and thought until he found the solution — to share his properties with poor people in his town. <u>All people were appreciated, in a</u> few months there were no more poverty in his town. ?

Everyone appreciated this

If the teacher is right about what the student wanted to write, this gives the student a clear model of one way of saying it. If the teacher is wrong, it makes clear to the student that a higher level of accuracy is needed if communication is to take place. It also encourages the student to try again to explain to the teacher what he or she did want to write. This explanation can take place at the beginning of the lesson while students try to correct their mistakes and the teacher walks round the class talking to individuals who want special help.

> Students often like this type of correction, because it concentrates on what they want to say, not on grammatical detail.

As with oral correction, we must not let the correction of linguistic detail discourage the students from wanting to express meanings that are important to them.

The importance of meaning

When we move beyond the writing of exercises and ask students to write more freely, there is one very important point to emphasise:

> If something is worth writing well, it's worth writing more than once.

Rewriting

I don't mean that students should be made to copy out lists of boring corrections. I mean that the teacher should make it clear to the students that it is very unusual for a writer simply to write something once and accept that first draft as the finished product. The first draft is written in order to be improved. (I can promise you that you are not reading the first draft of this book nor, in most places, the second draft, either!)

- So, first of all, we must ask students to write texts that are worth writing.
- Secondly, we must help them get used to the idea of the first writing being a draft for improvement.

> In this way, we can create a situation in which our marking becomes a helpful part of the writing process.

The chance to compare first and second drafts can help both student and teacher. A useful technique here is to ask students to write their first draft on the left hand page of an exercise book, and their second draft on the right hand page.

If we have to keep a record of regular grades for writing, then we can give these grades for the second draft, or make it clear to students that on some writing tasks we are not trying to teach them, just to test them. On test assignments, I would not use the ways of correction that we are discussing in this chapter, because I would want to make it clear to students when they are being taught and when they are being tested.

Inside this approach to the drafting of freer writing, then, there are two points that we need to keep in mind in addition to those we have already looked at:

- how ideas are connected beyond sentences;
- the importance of what the student wants to mean.

Ideas beyond sentences

When we mark a piece of writing, we have to treat it differently to a list of sentences. Here is one simple example:

He has worked in a factory for three years.

There is nothing wrong with this sentence, but I have taken it from a piece written by a student about his family:

Ref My sister is older than me. In my country, it is very difficult for a woman to get a good Job. He has worked in a factory for three years.

So, we have to look out for what words such as *he, she, it* and *they* refer to in a text. Sometimes the references may be a long way from each other and that is also when students most often make mistakes. One expects students to be able to self-correct this sort of mistake, so you might write *Ref.* in the margin as above, or just underline *He*, or ask the student to link up the reference like this:

My sister is older than me. In my country it is very difficult for a woman to find a good job. He has worked in a factory for three years.

Here is another sentence from one of my students that seems alright on its own:

However, the Ministry of Education has made English compulsory in secondary schools.

It comes, however, from this text:

All our schoolchildren want to learn English. However, the Ministry of Education has made English compulsory in secondary schools.

The student used the wrong word to link together these two ideas. When I read this, I just underlined *However*, because I expected the student to be able to self-correct, but in fact he couldn't. When we spoke about it at the beginning of the next lesson, it turned out that he thought that *however* meant the same as *therefore*.

It is clearly very important that students use such words to link their ideas together if they are to communicate what they want to mean. Let us look again at the example on page 58. We know that the writer's sister has worked in a factory, but what does that mean in this text? Are we to understand that his sister has done unusually well, or is this an example of the bad jobs that women get in his country? Which of the following two texts is what the student means?

My sister is older than me. In my country it is very difficult for a woman to find a good job, but she has worked in a factory for three years.

or

My sister is older than me. In my country it is very difficult for a woman to find a good job, so she has worked in a factory for three years.

So this is where we might put a $\wedge$ in the text and a C in the margin:

C   My sister is older than me. In my country it is very difficult for a woman to find a good job. $\wedge$ He has worked in a factory for three years.   *Ref*

> Correction means helping people to express themselves more accurately.

Let us look at one more example. Just before I started this section of the chapter, I wrote:
'...there are two points that we need to keep in mind...'

I wrote this because I think it helps the reader to follow what is coming. You know that there will be two points, not three or four. We need to teach students to use such organisational signals in their writing.

It is impossible to give examples of all the ways in which students can fail to organise what they want to mean. The general message is that teachers need to show students how to link their ideas together and organise their texts. Then we have to make this a part of the work we do when we help students improve their first drafts.

What the student wants to mean

If students are writing about something they are interested in, they will care about what they write. If the teacher's response is only in terms of linguistic correction, the students will quickly learn that even if the writing task appears interesting, the teacher really doesn't care what the students think about the topic.

> If the person I am writing for does not care what I write, why should I care myself? If I don't care what I am writing, I certainly don't care whether or not I express it accurately.

So, we need to show learners that we are interested in what they say by reacting to their ideas. We can write such comments as:

Good point!
That's interesting.
I can't agree with you here.
Yes, I feel that way sometimes.

on their work whether or not their idea is expressed linguistically accurately. If they see that we are reacting to their views, they will be encouraged to express them clearly.

Also, by commenting on the content of what students write, we can also help improve their writing. Look at this example:

People say that Japanese are very bad at learning
foreign languages. But foreigners are even worse at learning
Japanese.   *Have you any proof of this?*
The Japanese language...

By reacting to the content of what the student has written, the teacher is pointing out the need for some evidence at this stage of the text. Similarly, the teacher might indicate the need for an example, a reason, a result, a cause, a purpose, or whatever might be appropriate at a particular point in a text.

Here is another example:

My uncle likes baseball. This is very unusual in my country.

⌐*Say why*.

How will the student include this relevant information in the second draft?

With a relative clause?

My uncle, who lived in the U.S.A. for many years, likes baseball. This is unusual in my country.

With a subordinator?

Because he lived in the U.S.A. for many years, my uncle likes baseball. This is unusual in my country.

With a sentence connector?

My uncle lived in the U.S.A. for many years. As a result of this, he likes baseball, which is unusual in my country.

Clearly, there are many possibilities. The key point here is that the teacher, by suggesting the addition of certain information, is encouraging the student to become further involved in the use of the English language system.

> Reacting to the content of what students write is a positive way of helping them improve a draft of a text. In this way, it is an important part of correction.
>
> Reacting to content improves writing linguistically and gives encouragement. In this way, it is an important part of teaching.

Writing without correction

When we discussed the correction of oral English, we stressed the importance of encouraging the students to use the language fluently without correction. There are abilities which one can acquire only by a concentration on fluency. The same thing applies to writing, although many teachers feel less comfortable about it. We can think about this under three headings: expression, experiment and communication.

Expression

I once saw a teacher do this:

He put an apple, an orange and a banana on a table in the middle of the room. He told all the students to look at them for a few minutes and then write down six words that they had thought of while looking at the fruit. Then he asked the students to write down six words which described feelings they had experienced during the last week. Finally, he asked the students to write a poem of four lines, using the twelve words that they had listed. If they wanted to, students put their poems up on the wall so that others could read them.

Compared to standard English, there were some 'mistakes' in some of the poems, but it would have been very harmful to 'correct' these mistakes. That would be to take the view of mistakes that we criticised in Chapter 3. The students in this class were trying to express themselves in English, and this expression of self is what activities like the one above try to encourage.

> If learners can feel their own emotions being expressed in a language, this will build a relationship with the language which will help them learn it.

Experiment

Another teacher told me about a student who wrote:

I telephoned the office and a girl with a nylon voice answered.

The teacher could have underlined *nylon*, or suggested that the student meant *smooth*, but he didn't do either of these things. He left the sentence as it was, because this student was experimenting with the language.

> The wish to experiment is a good sign in a learner and should be encouraged. It shows an interest in the language and an enjoyment of it which will lead to learning.

Communication

Look at the following task, in which the students write letters as part of a communicative exchange. If the task is suitable for the students and well prepared, it can be fun. The students can enjoy making their requests and getting their answers.

Example 2

> Discuss these ideas with your teacher before you start writing.
>
> a) Write a letter on behalf of your class requesting permission from the town council to hold a barbecue in a local park. Then 'deliver' it.
>
> b) Write a letter to a friend who owns a country cottage, asking him if you can spend a weekend with some of your friends there. Then 'deliver' it.
>
> c) Read the letter you have received and reply to it as you think fit.

But if everything is always corrected, correction itself becomes the ultimate purpose of writing. Letters such as these can be left uncorrected as natural exchanges. If the receiver of the letter cannot understand something in it, then this will have to be clarified. If there is time, it can be useful and enjoyable to have this clarification carried out in writing. The students can use the kind of 'question mark' approach that I described above when responding to *attempts*.

> In any kind of activity where the students have to exchange written information in order to complete a task, it is the exchanging of this information that is important. Clarification may be necessary, but correction is not.

Some teachers insist that all written work must be corrected because writing is so permanent and students will learn what they see written down. There are two good arguments against this:

● Firstly, if students learned what they see written down, and if they learned so efficiently from constant correction, language teaching would be a lot simpler than it is.

- Secondly, this attitude continues to see correction as a matter of always comparing the student's English to an outside finished product, instead of seeing correction as a matter of helping people to develop their own accuracy.

We should be helping students to see their English as something which is developing and getting more and more useful. We have to make clear to them that when we don't correct something, this doesn't mean that it is necessarily absolutely standard English. It means that they should feel confident that they are making the right sort of progress.

> We are trying to make correction a part of the teaching and learning process, not something for learning to fight against.

Summary

1 Concentrate on the main point of an exercise, or on one or two types of mistake in less controlled writing.

2 Give time for self-correction and peer correction and help the students by showing where mistakes are and/or what kind of mistakes they have made.

3 Collect important mistakes for correction with the whole class.

4 React to the ideas that the students write and use them as a way of encouraging rewriting.

5 Not all written work should be corrected. The desire to express oneself, to experiment, and to communicate are more important to language learning than being absolutely correct.

Questions and activities

1 What can you remember about having your own written work marked and corrected?

2 Are there techniques in this chapter that you have already used? How do you feel about them?

3 Are there techniques in this chapter that you can't imagine using? Why?

4 What other techniques should be in this chapter?

5 Find an exercise that you will have to teach. Then write down some common mistakes that you would expect learners to make. Which of these mistakes would be worth correcting?

6 Take some examples of student writing and try marking selected mistakes with signals in the margin.

7 Where might you use the 'question mark' correction technique? What would you write?

8 If possible, discuss with language learners how they feel about the correction of their written work.

9 Try out a technique you haven't used before and discuss what happens.

References

Example 1   *Advanced Writing Skills* by J. Arnold and J. Harmer. p 17 (Longman 1978)

Example 2   *Functions of English* by L. Jones, p 43 (Cambridge University Press 1977)

Correctness and the teacher

The great majority of teachers of English in the world did not learn English as their mother tongue. They learned it at school, like their students. This brings with it a lot of advantages but, unfortunately, it also often brings a feeling of insecurity:

- Many teachers are embarrassed by the fact that their own English is not always free of mistakes.
- They are also concerned that, by making mistakes, they will give their students a bad model of the language.
- They are concerned that making mistakes will damage their status in their own eyes and in the eyes of their students.

The over-correct teacher

As a result of such feelings and worries, many teachers do not speak English freely in class. They speak carefully and slowly and only when they are reasonably sure that what they have prepared to say is correct.

This has a direct effect on the students. Students realise that what the teacher prizes above everything else is freedom from mistakes. So, they will respond to this. They will speak only when necessary and when they can avoid mistakes.

> Even if the teacher tells the students that they should try to express themselves freely, it will be difficult for the students to behave in this way when they see that it is not the teacher's way.

This is normal in life. When there is a contradiction between what someone says and what someone does, we tend to remember what that person does. So, there is a message here for the teacher and it is a difficult one:

> For the teacher, as for the students, there are times to concentrate on accuracy and times to concentrate on fluency.

If you are concentrating on presenting a new piece of language to the class, then of course you will want to present it accurately. If, however,

- you are telling a story,
- or organising an activity,
- or talking about a topic in a reading passage,
- or encouraging a discussion before a writing assignment,
- or talking about a film or a football match that you saw,
- or doing anything in English where it actually matters what you are saying,

you can best help your students by giving your attention to what you are saying and to fluent communication, not to linguistic detail.

The linguistic model

What about the question of the linguistic model? As far as students are concerned, a linguistic model has to come in the form of a person, a teacher.

The ideal model for them is a person from their own background who expresses himself or herself in English and who enjoys the language, using it forcefully and creatively with an emphasis on communication, not correctness, except when correctness is particularly important.

This is the type of linguistic model which is most likely to involve the students in using, and thus learning, the language. Students do not want to be, or to be mistaken for, foreign 'native speakers' of English.

> Students want to be themselves and to be able to express themselves in English.

Teacher status

The question of status is more difficult to answer, as it will be different in different countries. Some teachers do have 'native-like' command of English, but this is not the important point. If teachers insist that the native speaker is the best model for a teacher, then most teachers are immediately putting themselves in an inferior position as second-class speakers of the language.

If they then base their status on a pretence to be native-like speakers of the language, then they are creating for themselves a position of insecurity in which they will always feel threatened by their own performance.

> These teachers could base their status on the fact that they are successful examples of what their students aim to be: people from a shared background who have achieved an ability to communicate in English.

Most people want to learn English because it is a language of international communication. An international language has no native speakers. It is a language in which we try to communicate with each other as best we can. Native speakers of English also need help with this international form of communication. Once again, these are issues which can usefully be discussed with learners, if that is appropriate in a particular situation.

This chapter has dealt with the importance of fluency work by the teacher, even if the teacher cannot guarantee to be both fluent and accurate at the same time. This idea of balancing enjoyment and correctness is also a way of bringing this book to a close by returning to our original question.

Summarising activity

1 Write a list of points to summarise this chapter.

2 Discuss your summary of Chapter 8 with colleagues.

Conclusion: an answer

If making mistakes is a part of learning, and correction is a part of teaching, how do the two of them go together?

They go together in the work of teachers who see themselves as part of other people's learning, where the teaching exists to serve the learning. After all, we can learn without teachers, but we cannot teach without learners.

> Learners need a clear idea of the language that exists outside them, and a strong feeling that the language is developing inside them.

Students depend on a teacher to help with both of these needs, as the teacher decides, day after day, lesson after lesson, minute after minute:

- whether to correct,
- when to correct,
- what to correct,
- how to correct.

I hope that this book will help you with those decisions.

Suggestions for further learning

Four books on ELT methods with useful comments on correction:

DOFF, A *Teach English* (Cambridge University Press 1988)

GOWER, R AND WALTERS, S *Teaching Practice Handbook* (Heinemann 1983)

HARMER, J *The Practice of English Language Teaching* (Longman 1983)

HUBBARD, P, JONES, H, THORNTON, B, AND WHEELER, R *A Training Course for TEFL* (Oxford University Press 1983)

Specifically about mistakes and correction:

NORRISH, J *Language Learners and their Errors* (Macmillan 1983)

A reference book which describes mistakes typical of learners from different first language backgrounds:

SWAN, M AND SMITH, B *Learner English* (Cambridge University Press 1987)

Find out if there is a local library or teachers' centre that keeps magazines such as: *English Language Teaching Journal, Forum, Modern English Teacher, Practical English Teaching,* or perhaps a local English teachers' newsletter.

The best way of helping yourself develop as a teacher is to meet regularly with other teachers. There are also two major international ELT organisations that you might want to join:

IATEFL, 3 Kingsdown Chambers, Kingsdown Park, Tankerton, Whitstable, Kent, CT5 2DJ, England.

TESOL, Suite 205, 1118 22nd Street NW, Washington DC 20057, USA.